#Apenny4your
THOUGHTZ . . . .

#Apenny4your
THOUGHTZ . . . .

Dr. TL Penny

authorHOUSE®

AuthorHouse™
1663 Liberty Drive
Bloomington, IN 47403
www.authorhouse.com
Phone: 1-800-839-8640

First published by AuthorHouse   04/27/2012

ISBN: 978-1-4685-5462-5 (sc)
ISBN: 978-1-4685-5459-5 (e)

Library of Congress Control Number: 2012903149

Table Of Contents

DEDICATION

This Book is Dedicated to my Three girls Ashley (Ash) Kayla (K.K)
Rosanna (Rosie) and my Grandson Ashton (AJ) . . . . The four of
you are the Wind beneath my Wings. To my Armorbearer & friend
turned FAMILY forever, Lillie (Yibby), I Love you more than
ink and paper could ever convey! To my Two Wonderful Church
families in which I have the privilege of Pastoring, Shubach &
The Power Center Church, You are ALWAYS on my mind! . . . .
To my Mom, Judy Holt Findlay . . . . Yup! something good did
come out of Nazareth, lol, I love you mommy. And my Baby Sister
Takisha, You are such an encouragement to my life! I love you so
much! Well, I saved the BEST for last, I give all HONOR to my
Lord & Savior Jesus Christ, who gave me Hands and a Mind to
have even written this book, you have Been EVERYTHING to
me! And yes, I Love You even more than these!!! +TLP

FOREWORD

In today's society, we move so quickly. The pace of our lives is almost insane. We miss so much. One of the primary things that we miss is the time to receive and ponder the nuggets of wisdom falling from the lips of those who have had powerful encounters with God and carry His anointing. We are so privileged in this day to have a collection of spiritual wisdom, a trunk full of practical truth coming from the life, spirit and experience of Dr. T. L. Penny. The only hope we have of surpassing the state of our fathers is to build upon proven wisdom. Dr. Penny gives us the push that we need by filling this book with the kind of practical life-changing truths and humor that have elevated her above adversity and placed her on the forefront with others who are making a positive difference in this generation.

BISHOP ROSIE S. O'NEAL

Koinonia Christian Church, Greenville, N.C.

#Apenny4yourthoughtz

#Apenny4yourthoughtz: [*secretus*]-*Latin* for **secret**—set apart, withdrawn, hidden—For once you share a secret, though they may never tell a soul, you have now given the one in whom you've confided the power to become 'your' judge and jury . . . Ever wondered why Jesus told the lepers in Luke 5:14 not to tell anyone? Because he knew the treachery of humanity . . . some things people, are not worth the 'stroking of the emotions' or even the publications of a tell-all-book; some things should never be told to anyone but God, people have enough to say without giving them your 'secrets' . . . +TLP

#Apenny4yourthoughtz: The power of true wealth is not in the acquisition of money and things; but, in fact, the greatest currency available to humanity is simply 'information' . . . +TLP

#Apenny4yourthoughtz: [on social networking sites]While it is easy to make subliminal attacks through statuses, unfriending, and blocking . . . you exert way too much time thinking of whatever/whomever hurt or offended you; because 9 out of 10, you aren't on their minds anyway . . . soooooo, here's a better way: simply in Godly love walk away sweetly, softly, and quietly . . . .

("Smile and wave boy's, smile and wave") . . . knowing the inner, heartfelt truth that you never, ever have to communicate nor commune with them again, here or anywhere . . . . now go in peace and don't look back, you deserve it . . . +TLP

#Apenny4yourthoughtz: When people say they love you because you've done a lot for them or even because you were there when they needed you, count on them to stop 'loving' you when you stop doing for them or are unable to be there as before. Love should be unconditional . . . not chocked full of unrealistic terms and conditions . . . +TLP

#Apenny4yourthoughtz: Passionately driven and successful individuals know that there is no such thing as 'finish lines' in life, only in death . . . . .finish lines require hesitance and delay in speed and momentum, but the 'driven' just keep running and achieving until!!! . . . +TLP

#Apenny4yourthoughtz: Just because you can, doesn't mean you should . . . . choose to be in control! +TLP

#Apenny4yourthoughtz: Preachers listen, you don't have to 'drop names' to be accepted or respected, once 'you' finally figure out who you really are . . . +TLP

#Apenny4yourthoughtz: It's amazing how so many people in the church world will deliberately speak ill of you to those who inquire of you; perhaps to minister or simply just to meet you, they will place negative innuendos and speculation in their spirits to deter you from walking through those 'doors' . . . ironically enough, take a closer look at blockers, their ministries and lives for that matter, are either messy or at a standstill. If I've said it before, I've said it a million times, "What God has for me, it ain't for you!" . . . you can try to delay it, but you can't stop it . . . you know why? It's called, destiny . . . +TLP

#Apenny4yourthoughtz: You don't have to make a grand announcement that you are going to 'delete' folks out of your life . . . just simply a) stop calling them; b) stop answering their calls and responding to their emails, texts, Facebook, Twitter, etc. and lastly; c) don't speak of them or against them, because if they are truly 'deleted' they no longer exist! . . . www.invisibleYOU. com . . . +TLP

#Apenny4yourthoughtz: Let us always remember, that regardless of how anointed and gifted some of us within ministry are, it is never the responsibility of any church that we minister for to finance our lifestyle . . . www. maybegeta9to5.com . . . +TLP

#Apenny4yourthoughtz: Pastors, stop inviting people to your church, that would rather spend more time conversing with your people, but have very little to say to you . . . +TLP

#Apenny4yourthoughtz: What killed somebody else only made me mad . . . +TLP

#Apenny4yourthoughtz: When friends of your friend aren't friendly to you for no reason at all, check your'friend' . . . +TLP

#Apenny4yourthoughtz: Because we have a lot in common and get along well does not constitute that we should be friends; and, just because I don't hold conversation with you and we really don't have anything in common doesn't mean we're enemies . . . +TLP

#Apenny4yourthoughtz: If you never find fault in yourself, your desire for greatness will never be achieved . . . +TLP

#Apenny4yourthoughtz: What's worse than a liar is a person who believes that their lie is the truth . . . +TLP

#Apenny4yourthoughtz: Just as there are church members that privately say, "I'm praying as to whether to leave the ministry" . . . there are those of us in leadership saying, "Lord, please give them the ok" . . . +TLP

#Apenny4yourthoughtz: Time has taught me that just because they like your "ministry", (preaching, giftings), doesn't mean they like "you". Always remember, there are many that admire the roses, but don't care for the vase that holds them . . . don't be deluded . . . +TLP

#Apenny4yourthoughtz: Life is funny sometimes, you can have everything and still have nothing at all . . . +TLP

#Apenny4yourthoughtz: True and God ordained covenant relationships don't require you to feel guilty about your success; neither do they demand an explanation for the posture you must assume in order to maintain it . . . +TLP

#Apenny4yourthoughtz: When greeting leaders, don't try to shake and break their hands off like you're trying to shake or break them off; neither hug them so hard as to where they begin to lose oxygen, nor give them your life story in a two minute greeting . . . wisdom is key . . . +TLP

#Apenny4yourthoughtz: [Charismatics] we all love the Lord, but you might not want to go into An Acts 2 moment on a job interview, ignorance isn't related to the purposeful minsitry . . . +TLP

#Apenny4yourthoughtz: Listen! When you call someone on the phone and you ask if they're eating and they tell you something like "yes" as they are aggressively trying to chat and chew with you, please hang up right then! Don't cause people to develop G.E. R. D., (acid reflux), just because your toe hurts . . . let 'em eat, let 'em live . . . +TLP

#Apenny4yourthoughtz: If you have to coddle it to keep it, praise it to prove it, stay up all night to salvage it;

here's a word of wisdom, remove yourself completely away from it . . . . if it isn't a candy bar, rid yourself of the nuts . . . +TLP

#Apenny4yourthoughtz: Rejection is not someone releasing you out of their life; instead, it is you simply not letting them go while maintaining a mindset that they really want to stay, stop rejecting your TRUTH . . . +TLP

#Apenny4yourthoughtz: The Bible says in Psalm 30:5, "Weeping may endure for a night, but joy cometh in the morning" . . . just make sure that what had you weeping that "night", has been dispossessed by "morning", otherwise the cycle begins again . . . www. getoutandstayout.com . . . +TLP

#Apenny4yourthoughtz: Don't get overly excited when someone comes into your life and blesses you or even does you a kindness, often times it wasn't their idea in the first place: hard truth is, some of your greatest adversary's and potential haters were assigned by God to bless you; don't take it personal, don't get attached . . . they won't be staying for dinner!!! . . . +TLP

#Apenny4yourthoughtz: Sometimes when you say what you shouldn't have said and done what you should not have done, it can often times keep you from going where you would've gone . . . +TLP

#Apenny4yourthoughtz: "The autopsy is over, and I've dug a hole and buried it!" . . . +TLP

#Apenny4yourthoughtz: Have you ever noticed that when some people become elevated within ministry, they develop this weird English accent; I mean, outside of ministry they are ebonically literate all day . . . Lol! Seriously, then their vocals are decreased by ten octaves; they start sounding like Mr. Belvedere with a collar or big hat, lol! . . . Just thought I'd share . . . www. eitheryouisoryouaint.com . . . +TLP

#Apenny4yourthoughtz: Have you ever wondered how many of your Facebook friends on Facebook really even like you? . . . +TLP

#Apenny4yourthoughtz: Time has taught me that behind every smile and even one's laughter, is not necessarily happiness . . . +TLP

#Apenny4yourthoughtz: "Change does not denote failure" . . . +TLP

#Apenny4yourthoughtz: Are you WINfected? I am . . . . an unstoppable magnet that wins, and wins, and wins . . . . I am WINfected!!!! +TLP

#Apenny4yourthoughtz: I'm fueling my dreams with this declaration: "Yes, I've seen worse, but I've seen better too." . . . +TLP

#Apenny4yourthoughtz: Some of the greatest ministries in the world were not confined to four walls and a podium . . . a great mind and a strong relationship with God works just as well "without walls" . . . . +TLP

#Apenny4yourthoughtz: Cape Canaveral was only the launching pad, the think tank for the astronauts. I'm so glad they moved away from the "daydreamers" and actually shifted in their thinking and touched the moon . . . +TLP

#Apenny4yourthoughtz: Just because a decision one makes for themselves is not embraced by all, is not basis enough to still not make it . . . +TLP

#Apenny4yourthoughtz: I've come to learn that it is wasteful to invest long term goals, visions, and dreams into short term relationships . . . +TLP

#Apenny4yourthoughtz:SUCCESS....the accomplishment of an aim or purpose {S.U.C.C.E.S.S.} Succeeding Under Conditions and Circumstances when Everything Seems Stagnate . . . +TLP

#Apenny4yourthoughtz: Success may not happen overnight; but, one night, it will happen . . . +TLP

#Apenny4yourthoughtz: When your integrity speaks louder than your voice, then you're really saying something . . . +TLP

#Apenny4yourthoughtz: Maturity: When I was young, I couldn't wait to get the prize out of the Cracker Jack box; now that I am a bit older, the prize is simply an obstacle . . . +TLP

#Apenny4yourthoughtz: Many people pray . . . but the problem is that they act on their will and desire without waiting on a 'sure' answer from the lord . . . put a comma, not a period behind your petition; and wait, I say, wait . . . +TLP

#Apenny4yourthoughtz: Though one may not be your enemy, it certainly does not qualify them to be your 'friend' . . . +TLP

#Apenny4yourthoughtz: If the shoe fits wear it! If it doesn't, tap dance . . . +TLP

#Apenny4yourthoughtz: Funny thought: We'll trust the contents of a fortune cookie; yet, doubt God . . . +TLP

#Apenny4yourthoughtz: You are one of two things . . . either your biggest liability or your greatest asset, but only you have the power to choose . . . +TLP

#Apenny4yourthoughtz: Don't ever be afraid to edit or even delete what should have never been written into the script in the first place, "cut!" . . . +TLP

#Apenny4yourthoughtz: Don't just think in or out of the "box" . . . but take complete ownership of it . . . you've got the power!!! . . . +TLP

#Apenny4yourthoughtz: Everybody wants to be chief; but, please recognize there are some very successful Indians . . . +TLP

#Apenny4yourthoughtz: Sometimes when there is no response that is 'the' response . . . +TLP

#Apenny4yourthoughtz: Real friends speak without using words, hug without touching, and celebrate you when there is no party . . . got one? +TLP

#Apenny4yourthoughtz: Before entering another relationship; be it romantic or platonic, read the fine writing first! It's in the tone of their words . . . . think fast, move slow . . . +TLP

#Apenny4yourthoughtz: Love is what it says; then, turns around and does just what it said . . . +TLP

#Apenny4yourthoughtz: If your eyes can see it, and your mind can rationalize it, and your hands can hold it; then, it's not your destiny!!! . . . +TLP

#Apenny4yourthoughtz: If they can applaud you publically, but shun you privately; this, my dear friends, is not covenant . . . +TLP

#Apenny4yourthoughtz: When you really figure out who you are you'll have no problem saying, "No", without explanation . . . +TLP

#Apenny4yourthoughtz: Sometimes, you've just got to say, "Thank you for the door, but I've decided to take the window" . . . +TLP

#Apenny4yourthoughtz: If you place no value on yourself, your gifting, your ministry, or business, trust me when I tell you, no one else will . . . +TLP

#Apenny4yourthoughtz: The Bible says, "Time and chance happeneth to all . . . " So, we must be careful to discern, that every time opportunity or chance for an opportunity, does not always mean God has "favored" it . . . www.allthatglittersaintGod.com . . . +TLP

#Apenny4yourthoughtz: Don't allow years of painful rejection to cause you to accept just anything and everybody in your life now . . . www.beselective.com . . . +TLP

#Apenny4yourthoughtz: When something is broken, let God repair it, He won't end up cut and bleeding . . . He will fix it piece by PEACE . . . +TLP

#Apenny4yourthoughtz: Most people remain in your life, not because they love you, but because they love themselves . . . narcissism101 . . . +TLP

#Apenny4yourthoughtz: Love doesn't discriminate, it will fall into the arms of whomever will catch it! . . . +TLP

#Apenny4yourthoughtz: True covenant is never having to prove your friendship vocally . . . +TLP

#Apenny4yourthoughtz: Stop assuming that people feel about you, as you feel for them, just because they tell you they do with a smile . . . +TLP

#Apenny4yourthoughtz: Climate controls the productivity of one's harvest and health; hence, put a thermostat on some folks and turn them "off" . . . +TLP

#Apenny4yourthoughtz: We must never allow opportunity to override loyalty to leadership; and, any opportunity that challenges such loyalty is not an opportunity at all, but in fact outright rebellion . . . +TLP

#Apenny4yourthoughtz: Have you ever noticed that people actually become disappointed and angry when longtime rivals become friends? . . . +TLP

#Apenny4yourthoughtz: Everyone has a level of faithfulness; question is, however, to what? . . . +TLP

#Apenny4yourthoughtz: Just because your enemy smiles at you or even speaks to you is not necessarily a motion for reconciliation. Stop trying to recapture and reestablish nostalgic moments that once tried to destroy you. [Genesis 33:12-17] . . . +TLP

#Apenny4yourthoughtz: You are who you've been waiting for . . . +TLP

#Apenny4yourthoughtz: You cannot achieve complete and total closure until you completely and totally let go . . . +TLP

#Apenny4yourthoughtz: I'm thoroughly convinced that an assignment in a place can last for years; but, when it's over, it's over, and anything else you sow into it afterwards only becomes "dog food". (Mark 7:27) . . . +TLP

#Apenny4yourthoughtz: Once what you've been thinking one day becomes a "voice" . . . shift is INEVITABLE . . . +TLP

#Apenny4yourthoughtz: Ever wondered why it seems some get embraced and pushed more so in ministry or even in the workplace than others . . . here's why . . . intimidated people will never push or affirm what and who they think will surpass them or are as equally qualified as they are; so, they will always try to minimize or keep in the background greatness . . . but, it's ok because Samuel ain't leaving until David comes out! (1 Samuel 16:11) . . . +TLP

#Apenny4yourthoughts: Originality breeds perpetuality . . . +TLP

#Apenny4yourthoughtz: Beware of friendly enemies . . . +TLP

#Apenny4yourthoughtz: Why is it when there is talk about gifts within the kingdom we seem to find it necessary to associate them with TELEVISION as if this is the validating factor; guess what . . . there are some of the greatest gifts/voices in the body of Christ that have never been on any of these platforms, are they any less valuable? TV nor crowds make an individual noteworthy, it is their relationship with Christ and the power of the anointing working in their lives . . . . +TLP

#Apenny4yourthoughtz: Just because they are looking in your direction doesn't mean that they see you at all . . . +TLP

#Apenny4yourthoughtz: Knowing when to say nothing, is, within itself, a gift . . . +TLP

#Apenny4yourthoughtz: There is nothing that you do that God doesn't see . . . +TLP

#Apenny4yourthoughtz: Your BIG is still too small . . . +TLP

#Apenny4yourthoughtz: Tell the "comma" that "period" in your life is OVER . . . +TLP

#Apenny4yourthoughtz: You are not responsible for someone else's past, but you certainly have the power to endorse or not endorse their NOW . . . +TLP

#Apenny4yourthoughtz: Don't see everything you saw, and don't hear everything you heard . . . +TLP

#Apenny4yourthoughtz: The eyes are the lie detector of the soul . . . +TLP

#Apenny4yourthoughtz: If hell is a state of mind, some people are already there . . . +TLP

#Apenny4yourthoughtz: Prayer works by faith; so, if you are praying and asking God for something and you don't have any, you won't get it . . . +TLP

#Apenny4yourthoughtz: At some point you have to leave the pew . . . . and DO!!! . . . . +TLP

#Apenny4yourthoughtz: Money will only go as far as the holder takes it . . . +TLP

#Apenny4yourthoughtz: If you don't know me by now, you probably don't need to . . . +TLP

#Apenny4yourthoughtz: If they seem a little distant, perhaps they are . . . +TLP

#Apenny4yourthoughtz: The autopsy is over; now tag it and bag it ! . . . +TLP

#Apenny4yourthoughtz: When someone is holding a conversation with you and they say a vocabulary word you've never heard before, don't act like you understand it; stop them and ask, what does it mean . . . +TLP

#Apenny4yourthoughtz: What if your walls could talk? . . . +TLP

#Apenny4yourthoughtz: You know what's funny? The people that always say prayer changes things; they, themselves, never change . . . +TLP

#Apenny4yourthoughtz: You don't need a prayer partner until you have learned to first pray for yourself . . . +TLP

#Apenny4yourthoughtz: Pray without ceasing, but make certain that you cease, to pray . . . +TLP

#preacher2preacher

#preacher2preacher: Because this isn't your season of temptation, stop judging others, the wind blows in every direction . . . +TLP

#preacher2preacher: Because no one saw you do it doesn't mean you're innocent . . . have the same grace on others that God has bestowed upon you . . . why not cover their skeletons, since God covered and buried your corpses . . . +TLP

#preacher2preacher: I don't care how catchy the title sounds, don't preach it unless the text and the context emulates the title . . . +TLP

#preacher2preacher: Don't invite them if you don't like them . . . +TLP

#preacher2preacher: Please stop personalizing everybody you meet in the church world as your spiritual mother, father, big brother, little brother, big sister, little sister; some will never be anything to you but, "the brethren", and sometimes that's more than enough . . . +TLP

#preacher2preacher: Preachers the basis of the pulpit is for the Gospel to be preached, using life applications, practical principles, and sound doctrine, (not an invented one), etc . . . Not a place to bash your enemies and intimidate or humiliate the sheep . . . +TLP

#preacher2preacher: Roundtable discussions about leaders at the local restaurant, and sharing rumors or truths about the anointed of God, will only Give you indigestion for talking with your mouth full, but it won't deter their destiny at all . . . +TLP

#preacher2preacher: Stop watching other preachers' flyers and calling the churches they have been invited to trying to get an invitation by association or block the one who already has been invited . . . it's very distasteful . . . +TLP

#preacher2preacher: You should try studying, even when you haven't been asked to minister . . . +TLP

#preacher2preacher: Please pray for others, but put your name at the top of the list . . . +TLP

#preacher2preacher: Even if you have memorized the entire Bible it doesn't mean that you 'know' it . . . spend time with what you have read . . . +TLP

#preacher2preacher: We are never so modernized that we no longer take the Bible into the pulpit to minister . . . +TLP

#preacher2preacher: Don't wait until you're on your way into the pulpit to confess your sins to God . . . +TLP

#truthzBtold

#truthzBtold: Isn't it amazing how the Pentecostal church encourages you to become transparent and confess it all and the moment you do, you are ostracized or stagnated . . . we've got to do better, souls are depending on 'change' . . . +TLP

#truthzBtold: I don't care how Successful you are . . . for once people become 'common' with you no longer respect you it then will become impossible for them to respect your ministry, assignment, or gift . . . As much as you would love to embrace everybody, keep in mind that Christ didn't "hang" out with the multitude, and only 3 of His 12 disciples got close enough to really share in His pain and glory, and even one of them denied Him . . . . and even to them, He kept at a "stone's throw" . . . . Remember, everybody isn't qualified to "know" you . . . +TLP

#truthzBtold: It doesn't matter how successful you are or what you have acquired and achieved or how large or well known you or your ministry or business is: if you have a repugnant attitude or an arrogant disposition; though, you may "biblically" be loved, you will not "naturally" be liked . . . remember there's no nice in nasty . . . +TLP

#truthzBtold: Ever wonder why so many ministry gifts; though anointed, are so arrogant, conceited, and just plain 'ole nasty? I finally figured it out . . . the Church has given them that authority! By making them feel as if they are better than others, by giving them ridiculously large honorariums, several first class tickets, stretch limos, (with color preferences at that), hotel suites, etc . . . Yet, giving preachers that may not be as well known, but just as anointed, have integrity, and a pure heart an offering so small you can cash it at the local grocery store, Brother Bob's pick-up truck, and one ticket with a seat at the very back of the plane . . . They've made god's out of these vessels, but shift is coming and I pray that Dagon is ready! . . . ["And when they arose early on the morrow morning, behold, Dagon was fallen upon his face to the ground before the ark of the LORD; and the head of Dagon and both the palms of his hands were cut off upon the threshold; only the stump of Dagon was left to him." 1 Samuel 5:4]

#truthzBtold: Some of whom you hold nearest and dearest to the heart have become private enemies and are secretly trying to destroy your credibility and influence; all while saying, "I love you!" . . . +TLP

#truthzBtold: The only thing worse than a false prophet is a true prophet that hears from God, but will mingle "little" of what God say's with "most" of their own words and enticing speech just to keep doors open, in order to have the validation of people, and the approval of man . . . +TLP

#truthzBtold: Beware of "moment monsters" . . . . they come for one of three reasons; to take your place, share your place, or distract you until you're out of place . . . . everybody that is supposedly supporting your party, revival/conference, or just your special moment, is not always there genuinely with you in mind; but, in fact, with themselves in mind, and what they can extract or detract from your moment . . . . truth be told . . . . they hate the fact that it is you, and not them . . . +TLP

#truthzBtold: Although you must forgive it, if you can't forget it . . . it then becomes a conflict allowing it to remain . . . +TLP

#fashionCENTSLESS

#fashionCENTSLESS: If your mobile phone is bigger than our house phone, I wouldn't ever take it out in public, lol . . . +TLP

#fashionCENTSLESS: Please take the tag off of your suit / coat sleeve; and, when wearing a shirt and tie, please don't wear a chain with a charm on the top of the tie . . . . and while we're redefining . . . . lose the white-tube-socks-with-dress-shoes on Sunday mornings . . . this very well could have been your hold up . . . . of what, you may ask? . . . . probably EVERYTHING . . . +TLP

#youmightneedapedicure: *if the camera crew of* Ripley's *Believe It or Not* shows up at your pedicure station asking for an interview . . . +TLP

#youmightneedapedicure: If your tech has to file a Worker's Comp. Claim after doing your feet . . . +TLP

#youmightneedapedicure: If your nail the puts on baseball mitts instead of latex gloves to do your feet . . . +TLP

#youmightneedapedicure: If you are accused of making scuff marks on the kitchen floor and you have been bare-footing it all day . . . lol . . . +TLP

#youmightneedapedicure: If your technician gets a pair of hedge clippers and a can of paint to do your feet . . . lol . . . +TLP

#RaNdOmthoughtz

#RaNdOmThOuGhTz: . . . **Stable Mind:** Here's what I know . . . church folk that act "holier" than thou, are the ones that have the biggest stains . . . +TLP

#RaNdOmThOuGhTz: Stable mind . . . you've ever heard folks say stuff like, "I've got a bad feeling", or "something doesn't feel right in my spirit" . . . . well, guess what . . . . sometimes it's just mixed up food that hasn't digested properly . . . . getthelittlepurplepill. com . . . . +TLP

#RaNdOmThOuGhTz: Stable mind: Have you noticed that some pastors act like funeral directors and some funeral directors act like pastors? +TLP

#RaNdOmThOuGhTz: Stable mind: . . . Butter crème frosting tastes so much better than whipped frosting . . . +TLP

#RaNdOmThOuGhTz: Stable mind: Is it me, or does home-cooked food taste better after a good church service? +TLP

#RaNdOmThOuGhTz: Stable mind: I am vintage, are you? Characterized by excellence, maturity, and enduring appeal; classic, original . . . +TLP

#RaNdOmThOuGhTz: Stable mind: I wonder whether "Angry Birds" . . . would be considered cruelty to animals . . . . +TLP

#RaNdOmThOuGhTz: Stable mind: You know it dawned on me that I've never joined the church that I pastor, lol . . . +TLP

#pEtpEEves: Don't you just hate it . . . when you're eating and someone puts their fork or spoon in your plate? +TLP

#pEtpEEves: Don't you just hate it . . . when there are at least 4 other chairs in the room, but someone will come and sit right next to you . . . +TLP

#pEtpEEves: It really agitates me when I see someone reading a novel and their lips are moving at the same time . . . +TLP

Dr. TL Penny

#pEtpEEves: Reading is a wonderfully subtle activity that basically suggests, "I'd like to be left alone". . . soooooo, don't you just hate it when you're in the middle of reading a good book and someone stops you and asks, "So, what's happening in your book, and what chapter are you in now?". . . . lol. +TLP

Bonus: **YoUCaNALWaYztEll:** Have you ever met someone and you both hit it off from the start, I mean really connected . . . . then, the next time you speak to them they act a bit distant . . . not so friendly, I believe the street term is "shady" . . . most times, someone has gotten in their ear and sowed a negative seed about you . . . . and it is sad, because these vultures will destroy potentially great alliances and friendships . . . but, it's ok, because at the end of the day you don't need anyone in your life without spiritual discernment and, quite frankly, that shallow minded . . . +TLP